AF228436

GALATIANS–
2 THESSALONIANS

GALATIANS–
2 THESSALONIANS

Rob Wynalda, Joel R. Beeke,
and Paul M. Smalley

REFORMATION HERITAGE BOOKS
Grand Rapids, Michigan

Reformation Heritage Books
3070 29th St. SE
Grand Rapids, MI 49512
616-977-0889
orders@heritagebooks.org
www.heritagebooks.org

25 26 27 28 29 30/11 10 9 8 7 6 5 4 3 2

ISBN 979-8-88686-170-9

PREFACE

In Deuteronomy 17, Moses leaves final instructions concerning the future of Israel. As a prophet of God, he foretells that Israel will set a king over the nation (v. 14). This king must be an Israelite, not a foreigner (v. 15), and is forbidden to do certain things (vv. 16–17). In verse 18, Moses transitions to what the king should do. The king is commanded not to simply acquire a copy of the law (the entire book of Deuteronomy), but to handwrite his own copy of the law. The purpose was so that he would read it, fear the Lord, obey, avoid pride, not deviate, and enjoy a long reign (vv. 19–20; cf. Prov. 4:20–27).

More than three thousand years later, modern educators have discovered that students who write out notes by hand have a much higher retention rate than those who simply hear or visually read the information. Apparently, God knew this to be true for the kings of Israel also.

This series of books, known as The Bible Journal, was born from the insight found in Deuteronomy 17:18. Your Bible Journal gives you the opportunity to write out your own copy of a portion of the Holy Scriptures, just as the ancient kings of Israel were instructed to do. Writing out the words of the Bible helps a person to engage the Word of God by slowing down the process of reading the text. Writing answers to the discussion questions also helps you to thoughtfully engage the text. Furthermore, by completing a journal, you leave a legacy to pass on to future generations your insights and personal applications of the text (Deut. 6:6–9; Ps. 78:4–7).

To prepare you to meditate on this portion of the Holy Scriptures, we include an introduction to the book of the Bible to help you understand more thoroughly the Bible book you are about to write out in full. Study Questions and Devotional Reflections have been added after the blank pages set aside for copying each chapter of God's Word. The Study Questions focus on individual verses to keep you thinking about what you are writing, and the Devotional Reflections are designed to help you focus on a few of the major takeaways for your practical Christian life that each Bible chapter provides. We wish to thank Reformation Heritage Books for allowing us to use material drawn from *The Reformation Heritage KJV Study Bible* for the Bible Introduction material and for the Devotional Reflections. The Study Questions have been written by the authors of *The Bible Journal*. Thus, The Bible Journal walks you through a process of getting acquainted with a book of the Bible, copying a chapter by hand, reflecting on the meaning and application of that chapter, and then repeating the process for the next chapter. Families, friends, and small groups can work through a journal together, discussing their meditations for mutual edification as guided by the discussion questions.

The mass production of the Bible since the invention of the printing press has greatly blessed the world. However, there is also great benefit for Bible readers of all ages in following the Deuteronomy 17:18 principle and producing your own handwritten copy of the text.

May God richly bless you in writing and learning His Word through The Bible Journal (Rom. 1:16).

—Rob Wynalda, Joel R. Beeke, and Paul M. Smalley

Introduction to the Book of
GALATIANS

AUTHORSHIP: Pauline authorship of Galatians is clearly stated (1:1–2; 5:2). Furthermore, it has been advocated and defended throughout church history. The earliest writings of various church fathers (e.g., Clement of Rome, Ignatius, Polycarp, Justin Martyr) contain frequent references to Galatians and to Paul's authorship. Pauline authorship has been almost universally maintained. No convincing arguments have been produced by those who have denied it.

DATE: The date of Galatians has been intensely debated. Though some advocate a later date (AD 57–58), the earlier date (AD 48–49) is preferable. First, in 2:1–10 Paul refers to a visit to Jerusalem, when he met with certain men who were leaders. While some see this visit corresponding to the Jerusalem Council (Acts 15:1–4), it is more likely that this visit was for the famine relief visit to Jerusalem (Acts 11:30), which occurred approximately AD 47. This indicates that the epistle was written sometime after Paul's first missionary journey that preceded the Jerusalem Council. Second, while some argue that "at the first" in Galatians 4:13 refers to Paul's second missionary journey (Acts 16:6), this is not necessary as the Greek could simply indicate "previously." It is therefore probable that Paul is referring to his visit to South Galatia (Acts 14:21), which occurred before the Jerusalem Council. Third, the epistle was written soon after the conversion of the Galatians (Gal. 1:6). Paul was amazed, not only at the fact that the Galatians were moving away from the Lord, but that they were moving away "so soon." In light of these facts, it is preferable to assign an early date of AD 48–49 for the composition of Galatians.

Likewise, who these Galatians were to whom Paul is writing has also been vigorously debated. The letter is addressed to "the churches of Galatia" (1:2) and the "Galatians" (3:1). The contention is whether this is a territorial or ethnic identification. Ethnically, Galatia would refer to the territory where the Gauls or Celts dwelt after their invasion of Central Europe in 278 BC. If Paul is addressing the ethnic people, the letter would be addressed to the cities of Ancyra, Pessinus, and Tavium—the northern Galatia territory. If Paul is addressing the territory, it is the Roman province of Galatia, which would indicate the cities in southern Galatia of Antioch of Pisidia, Iconium, Lystra, and Derbe. We know that Paul visited these cities in his first missionary journey.

While the arguments are complex, it is probable that Paul is addressing the southern Galatians and therefore Galatia should be understood as a territory. This is likely for several reasons. First, Paul knew the readers personally (Gal. 1:8; 4:11–15, 19). Second, the route listed in Acts 16:6 and 18:23 appears to be through south Galatia. Third, Paul typically used the Roman designation of provinces. Fourth, Galatia contributed to the relief fund (1 Cor. 16:1), with persons from southern Galatia accompanying the transport of the gift (Acts 20:4). Fifth, Barnabas is mentioned three times in Galatians (Gal. 2:1, 9, 13), intimating that the readers knew Barnabas. Barnabas, however, only journeyed with Paul on his first missionary journey. For these reasons, it is likely that Paul is addressing those in southern Galatia.

THEME: Salvation is by the free grace of God received through faith in the righteousness of Christ apart from any works of the law.

PURPOSE: First, to emphasize again the very heart of the gospel, justification by faith alone in Christ's righteousness apart from the works of the law. Second, to call the Galatian Christians to prove the reality of their spirituality through living by faith in Christ, a life in which the fruit of the Spirit would abound. Third, to destroy the message of the Judaizers by showing that it was a false gospel.

SYNOPSIS

The Contribution of Galatians to Redemptive Revelation
The writing of this letter was occasioned by the insidious influence that was being exerted upon the Galatian churches by the dangerous teaching of the Judaizers. They were arguing that to be truly saved, one who professed faith in Christ also had to submit to circumcision and indeed to the entire Jewish ceremonial law. This was the heresy that the Jerusalem Council would later address (Acts 15), though it would continue to trouble the churches.

With apostolic authority (Gal. 1:1, 11–12) and loving directness (v. 6; 4:12–20), Paul sets forth the exclusive claims of the gospel against any mixture of law and gospel in justification. Even if an angel of light taught any other thing than the gospel of God which Paul had brought, to leave the gospel would bring a curse (1:8–9; 3:10), from which Christ delivers all those who believe (3:13–14). By faith we are united to Christ, his death and resurrection (2:19–20; 5:24). The giving of the Mosaic law had not undone the doctrine of justification by faith alone as was seen in Abraham, the father of the faithful (3:7–9, 15–18), but rather served as a schoolmaster to bring to Christ (vv. 19–25). Those who have believed will prove the genuineness of their faith through living by faith in Christ (2:20), thus living a life that shows the fruit of the Spirit (5:22–24; 6:8). There is no other way of acceptance with God apart from the cross of Christ and faith in His merit (2:16, 21; 6:14).

OUTLINE
I. Introduction (1:1–5)

II. Defense of Paul's Apostleship (1:6–2:21)
    A. Paul's Gospel Is True (1:6–10)
    B. Paul's Calling to the Gospel (1:11–24)
        1. Christ Revealed in Paul (1:11–17)
        2. Paul's Early Ministry (1:18–24)
    C. Paul's Confirmation by the Apostles (2:1–10)
    D. Paul's Conflict with Peter (2:11–21)
        1. Paul Opposed Peter (2:11–14)
        2. Christ's Death Effectual in Paul (2:15–21)

III. Proclamation of Justification (3:1–5:12)
    A. Receiving the Spirit by Faith (3:1–6)
    B. Justification by Faith Alone (3:7–29)
        1. Scriptural Verification (3:7–14)
        2. Human Example (3:15–18)
        3. Law and Faith (3:19–29)
    C. Sonship Is by Faith (4:1–7)
    D. Blessings Come by Faith (4:8–31)
    E. Endurance through Faith (5:1–12)

IV. Revelation of Life in the Spirit (5:13–6:10)
    A. Walking by the Spirit (5:13–26)
    B. Serving One Another (6:1–10)

V. Closing (6:11–18)

Notes

1

2

3

4

5

6

7

8

Notes

9

10

11

12

13

14

15

Notes

16

17

18

19

20

21

22

23

24

STUDY QUESTIONS

1. Verse 1: What does Paul say about his calling to be an apostle? Why is that important as he addresses false teaching in Galatia?

2. Verse 4: What are three reasons Christ gave His life?

3. Verses 8–9: What does Paul say about anyone, even an angel, who preaches a false gospel?

4. Verses 11–12: How did Paul learn the gospel that he preached?

5. Verses 15–16: How was Paul converted?

6. Verses 18–19: Why did Paul insist he had limited contact with other apostles (vv. 11–12)?

7. Verses 22–24: How did the churches of Judea respond to news about Paul's activities?

DEVOTIONAL REFLECTIONS

1. The surest protection from the false gospel is a fresh and clear reminder of the true gospel. This Paul does in his opening greeting in verses 3–5, in which he gives a succinct summary of the victorious deliverance that flows from Christ's atoning sacrifice. Meditate on this true gospel, and praise God for it.

2. There can be no compromise with those who pervert the gospel of Christ. Paul not only brands the false gospel as a perversion of the true, he also by inspiration reveals that those who promote another gospel will be damned. Thus there can be no fellowship with such men. Why is separation from preachers of a false gospel absolutely imperative?

3. The conversion of those who were formerly opponents of the gospel brings great glory to the Lord. Paul, the former blasphemer and persecutor, goes into much detail to show the reality of his conversion so that the very people he had persecuted glorified God for the change they saw in him. For what enemies of the gospel do you pray?

Notes

1

2

3

4

5

6

Notes

7

8

9

10

11

12

13

Notes

14

15

16

17

18

19

Notes

20

21

STUDY QUESTIONS

1. Verse 2: What prompted Paul to go to Jerusalem with Barnabas (Acts 11:27–30)?

2. Verses 3–5: Why was Titus pressured to be circumcised? How did Paul respond?

3. Verse 9: How did James, Cephas (Peter), and John receive Paul and Barnabas?

4. Verses 11–14: What did Paul later do to Peter? Why?

5. Verse 16: What does "justify" mean (see Deut. 25:1; Prov. 17:15)? How is a sinner justified by God?

6. Verse 20: How does being united to Christ transform a person's life?

7. Verse 21: What would be true if we could be justified by obeying the law?

1. The Christian should make every effort to remove all doubts about his or her profession of the gospel. Paul knew that his enemies had slandered him before his fellow apostles, thus when he went to Jerusalem he carefully showed them that he believed and preached the same gospel as they did. It is always good to remove all suspicion from our names, if possible, remembering that it is only in Christ that believers are justified.

2. Sometimes even the rebuking of a fellow believer is necessary in order to defend the gospel. At Antioch Paul had to withstand Peter because his action in separating from the Gentiles endangered the truth of justification through Christ alone. But Peter did not resent the rebuke, later referring to Paul as a "beloved brother" (2 Peter 3:15). Do you welcome correction and reproof as David did (Ps. 141:5)?

3. Believers live the Christian life in the same manner as they commence it. This is Paul's triumphant assertion in verse 20. The believer is in union with Christ and by faith draws from Him all that is needed to live the life of the believer in a sinful world. Reflect on the all-powerful and ever-fresh gospel of Christ's death for sinners.

Notes

1

2

3

4

5

6

7

Notes

8

9

10

11

12

13

14

Notes

15

16

17

18

19

20

Notes

21

22

23

24

25

26

27

28

29

STUDY QUESTIONS

1. Verse 2: How do people receive the Holy Spirit (v. 14)?

2. Verse 6: How was Abraham counted righteous before God?

3. Verses 8–9: Who receives the blessing promised to Abraham?

4. Verse 10: What does the law do to those who do not completely obey it?

5. Verses 13–14: How are sinners released from God's curse and given His blessing?

6. Verse 16: Who is the great "Seed," or offspring, of Abraham?

7. Verse 19: Why did God add the law of Moses to the promise given to Abraham?

8. Verse 24: What is one purpose of God's law? How does it do that?

9. Verses 26–28: What new identity is given to all believers in Christ?

10. Verse 29: Who are the heirs of God's promise to Abraham?

DEVOTIONAL REFLECTIONS

1. It is imperative to guard against all that would take away our confidence in Christ alone in the Christian life. Spiritual growth and maturity are never enhanced by reliance on the efforts of the flesh. How can Christians drift away from complete dependence on Christ?

2. The penalty of the law is its dreadful curse—the sentence of death. Thus, for sinners to be freed from that curse and to be justified before the law that demands it, Christ became a curse for them! Let no child of God ever forget what Christ endured.

3. No sinner is ever justified by the law, but not because there is any fault in the law. The fault lies in the sinner, namely, in his inability to give the perfect obedience the law requires. But the inflexible demands of the law cause it to become a means of bringing the sinner to faith in Christ's perfect obedience by which the law was satisfied. Do you rest in Christ alone for God's acceptance?

Notes

1

2

3

4

5

6

7

8

Notes

9

10

11

12

13

14

15

16

Notes

17

18

19

20

21

22

23

24

Notes

25

26

27

28

29

30

31

STUDY QUESTIONS

1. Verses 1–3: What was the status of believers before Christ came?

2. Verses 4–5: What does Paul teach about the person and mission of Christ?

3. Verse 6: What does Paul teach about the person and mission of the Holy Spirit?

4. Verse 10: What concerned Paul about their view of the calendar? Why (Col. 2:16–17)?

5. Verses 14–15: How much had the Galatians loved and respected Paul?

6. Verse 19: How does Paul describe his ministry? What does this teach us?

7. Verses 22–23: What does Paul recount about Abraham (Gen. 21:1–13)?

8. Verse 24: What do these two women represent?

9. Verse 27: What Scripture passage does Paul quote?

10. Verse 29: What do the two children represent?

DEVOTIONAL REFLECTIONS

1. Christ's first coming was an astounding miracle, for it was the appearance of the God-man. God sent forth His Son—there is His deity. He was made of a woman—there is His humanity. But the two natures are united in the one person; thus, He is the God-man. Great is the mystery of redemption! Dwell on this truth: "God was manifest in the flesh" (1 Tim. 3:16).

2. We must agonize over those who are endangered by another gospel. Paul had labored hard and suffered much to see the Galatians converted to Christ. But he was prepared to go through labor pains again to see them recovered from the soul-destroying message of the Judaizers. Let us labor by grace to see those who are deluded cast aside the lie. Whom do you know in this position? How do you labor for them?

3. It is vital for the Christian to know the Scriptures. Note Paul's use of the Word of God as he reasons with the Galatians: "Do ye not hear the law?" (v. 21); "For it is written" (v. 22); "Nevertheless what saith the scripture?" (v. 30). Is Scripture the only compass by which you navigate daily?

Notes

1

2

3

4

5

6

7

8

9

Notes

10

11

12

13

14

15

16

17

18

19

20

21

22

23

24

25

26

1. Verse 1: What must Christians stand against? How do they do that?

2. Verses 3–4: What is the result of trying to be justified by obedience to God's law?

3. Verses 5–6: What is crucial to Christianity instead of circumcision?

4. Verse 11: What would happen if Paul preached circumcision? Why?

5. Verse 14: In what precept is the law fulfilled?

6. Verse 17: What conflict rages inside of the believer?

7. Verses 19–21: What are the works of the flesh?

8. Verses 22–23: What is the fruit of the Spirit?

9. Verse 25: What is the responsibility of those to whom the Spirit gives life?

DEVOTIONAL REFLECTIONS

1. The Christian's liberty in Christ is the means whereby he stands fast against all that would enslave. The goal of the Enemy is to bring the believer into spiritual bondage, thereby robbing the soul of enjoyment in Christ. But his defense is the very liberty he has in Christ. Christ sets believers free from the law's demand for perfect obedience by giving that perfect obedience on our behalf, forming the basis for their justification and thus the basis for standing fast against all that would enslave. Do you know this struggle personally? To whom do you look for defense and liberty?

2. Christian liberty is freedom from sin and condemnation, and freedom to serve Christ. Some teach that the believer's liberty in Christ is freedom from God's moral law as a direction for how to live, thus granting freedom to indulge fleshly appetites. This antinomian heresy must be resisted vigorously. The liberty to which we have been called is not license to sin but freedom to obey Christ and do His will. Why is it the Christian's liberty to serve others in love?

3. The justified man produces true holiness because he has the Holy Spirit within. Justification is always followed by sanctification; and sanctification is by the Spirit, not by the law. The Spirit is God's gift to the Christian on the basis of the merit of Christ. By the Spirit's work in the heart the believer is made holy, demonstrated by the fruit that the Spirit produces. Why is it crucial that we remember that sanctification is by grace alone?

Notes

1

2

3

4

5

6

7

8

Notes

9

10

11

12

13

14

15

Notes

16

17

18

STUDY QUESTIONS

1. Verses 1–2: How should the church respond when a believer falls into sin?

2. Verse 6: What should Christians do for those who teach them the Word?

3. Verse 9: What can motivate believers to do good to others?

4. Verses 12–13: Why did some people require circumcision?

5. Verse 14: In what should believers boast? Why?

6. Verse 15: What really matters instead of circumcision?

DEVOTIONAL REFLECTIONS

1. A ministry of restoration can only be exercised by believers who are spiritually strong. Paul's injunction is that those who are spiritual are to restore the one who is caught off guard and falls into sin. The inference is that the ministry of restoration can only be exercised by believers who themselves are on their guard. One of the marks of spiritual strength is a cautiousness so as to avoid every pit that Satan digs, into which the careless will fall (Jude 23). Should this not move us to pray earnestly that we might be kept from falling?

2. Spiritual increase will come at God's appointed time. Paul states that "in due season we shall reap" (v. 9). The word for "season" refers to a fixed or appointed time, signifying that the Lord has times appointed when spiritual reaping will take place. It is such a truth that actually is the means of keeping us from fainting and growing weary in the lengthy times of sowing the spiritual seed. Ultimately our "harvest time" is Christ's coming. How can you rest more in God's appointed time for all things?

3. The one matter in which the believer may rightfully boast is the work of Christ. Paul repudiates all thoughts of glorying or boasting in anything except "the cross," the finished work of Christ. In that work no man had any part, for Christ alone was qualified to make satisfaction for sin. Therefore, in the work of the cross the believer may boast without sinning. What is it about the cross that excites the Christian to rejoice, exalt, and praise the Lord?

Introduction to the Book of
EPHESIANS

AUTHORSHIP: No one in the early church questioned that Paul wrote this epistle. However, some modern scholars argue that another author wrote in Paul's name. They say: (1) Ephesians has a different style and vocabulary than Paul's letters. (2) Ephesians goes beyond Paul's theology in its view of church and marriage, and fails to include his characteristic emphasis on Christ's future coming. (3) Ephesians is somewhat similar to Colossians, thus proving that it was written by someone imitating Paul's style. (4) Another author could have used Paul's name in order to honor him, employing a pseudonymous style acceptable among early Christians.

In response to these arguments, we can say that: (1) An author can be quite versatile in his style and vocabulary as he writes on different occasions. Writings as short as the New Testament epistles do not give us a large enough sample of an author's writings to draw fine lines about distinctive style and vocabulary. (2) No single epistle of Paul captures all of his teachings, so we should not be surprised that Ephesians adds some insights to what we find in his other writings, while not contradicting them. Nor does it neglect Paul's great themes. For example, this epistle says much about the hope of Christ's coming (1:10–11, 14, 18; 2:7; 4:4, 10, 13, 30; 5:5–6, 27; 6:8). (3) The similarities of Ephesians to Colossians are fascinating but can be explained by the same author addressing two churches in different situations. (4) Impersonating an apostle was not acceptable in the early church. Both Tertullian and Serapion of Antioch bore witness that the church rejected writings falsely claiming to be written by apostles.

The epistle itself testifies that it was written by "Paul, an apostle of Jesus Christ" (1:1). In the midst of the epistle, the author refers to himself as "I Paul, the prisoner of Jesus Christ" (3:1). He also writes of his supernatural calling as an apostle to the Gentiles (vv. 5–8). If the author was not the apostle Paul, then he was guilty of gross deception. Indeed, he would be a hypocrite of the worst kind, for he urged the Ephesians to put away lying and speak the truth (4:25). Such accusations are unworthy of this noble epistle. On the contrary, Ephesians bears the marks of being divine revelation, the Word of the God who cannot lie (Rom. 3:4; Titus 1:2). Therefore we have every reason to accept it for what it claims to be: the epistle of the apostle Paul.

DATE: Paul said that he wrote as a prisoner in chains (3:1; 4:1; 6:20). Paul was imprisoned many times (2 Cor. 11:23), but his major imprisonments took place in Caesarea from AD 57–59 (Acts 23:33; 24:27), and in Rome from AD 60–62 (Acts 28:30). Tradition holds that he wrote this epistle from Rome. It seems likely that Ephesians was written during the same imprisonment as Colossians, since they have similar messages; both speak of his imprisonment (Col. 4:3, 10, 18), and both were delivered by Tychicus (Eph. 6:21; Col. 4:7).

THEME: God's riches of grace in Christ for His body.

PURPOSE: To teach believers about the glorious riches which belong to them by their union to the crucified and resurrected Lord Jesus, and to call them to walk worthy of their privileges by vital church membership, lifelong repentance, well-ordered households, and spiritual combat against the Devil. Unlike some epistles, Paul does not address any specific spiritual dangers threatening the church. Instead, he writes to strengthen a healthy church. If we may deduce Paul's purpose from his prayers for the church, then he wrote to the Ephesians in order to lead them into a richer experiential knowledge of their Savior in the context of their everyday lives in a fallen world.

SYNOPSIS
The Contribution of Ephesians to Redemptive Revelation
Ephesians presents theology as doxology, that is, the truth of God for the worship of God. It is a book resounding with praise for the riches of God in Christ. His death (1:7; 2:13–16; 5:2, 25) and exaltation (1:20–22; 2:5–6; 4:8–10) are the means to salvation for all those united to Him. In Him believers have every spiritual blessing (1:3), riches of grace (vv. 7, 18; 3:8) overflowing from God's great love for His people (2:5). Paul strains language to express the inexpressible glory of God (1:19; 2:7; 3:20), which comes through Christ in fullness (1:23; 3:17; 4:10, 13; 5:18). God's riches for His people consist particularly of the Holy Spirit in all His gifts and fruit (1:13–14, 17; 2:18, 22; 3:5, 16; 4:3–4, 30; 5:9, 18; 6:17–18). The book is profoundly shaped by the doctrine of the Trinity, as Father, Son, and Holy Spirit operate in harmony to save a people for God's glory.

Thus Ephesians has much to say about the church, the body, and the bride of Jesus Christ (1:1, 18, 23; 2:19–22; 3:6, 15, 21; 4:4–16; 5:23, 25–27, 29–32; 6:18). They are nothing less than the temple of the living God and the showcase of God's glory. As a people of amazing privilege, they have a high calling to fulfill (4:1). This calling places ethical obligations upon every dimension of life, as Paul makes clear in the second half of the epistle. The body must be united in love and the saints must be holy in conduct (chs. 4–5). The church must be a light exposing the corruptions of the world (5:7–14) and a spiritual army standing in righteousness against the demonic forces of evil (6:10–18).

This strong moral thrust finds its footing in the doctrines of salvation by grace alone (chs. 1–2). Though Christians were once as the rest of the world, dead in sin, dwelling in spiritual darkness, and doomed to suffer God's wrath (2:1–3; 4:17–19; 5:5–6), God has given His people forgiveness and life, a life shaped and energized by the gospel of Jesus Christ. They are the people in union with Christ, and this union, expressed in the frequent "in him" or "with him," is central to Paul's message. It is the "mystery of the gospel" (6:19), that is, the secret truth planned by God in eternity and now revealed. The mystery is that God is joining people from all nations to His Son in order to enjoy His redemptive love and share in His exaltation as head over all things (1:9–10; 3:3–6, 9; 5:29–32). Thus, Ephesians reveals the riches of God's grace in Christ to Christ's body, the elect from Jew and Gentile. It is a book of salvation by grace alone, in Christ alone, for the glory of God alone.

OUTLINE

I. Greetings: Grace and Peace (1:1–2)

II. The Doctrine of God's Grace in Christ for His Body (1:3–3:21)
    A. The Praise of God's Grace in Christ (1:3–14)
    B. The Power of God's Grace in the Risen Lord (1:15–2:10)
    C. The Peace of God's Grace in the Crucified Lord (2:11–22)
    D. The Purpose of God's Grace Revealed in Christ (3:1–21)

III. The Calling to Walk as the Body of Christ (4:1–6:22)
    A. Walk Worthy as One Body (4:1–16)
    B. Walk in the New Man, Not in the Old Ways of Sin (4:17–5:14)
    C. Walk in God's Wisdom for Relationships (5:15–6:9)
    D. Walk in the Lord's Armor for Spiritual Warfare (6:10–22)

IV. Concluding Blessing: Peace and Grace (6:23–24)

Notes

1

2

3

4

5

6

7

8

Notes

9

10

11

12

13

14

15

Notes

16

17

18

19

20

21

22

23

STUDY QUESTIONS

1. Verse 3: Why should the saints bless (or praise) God?

2. Verses 4–5: Why has God blessed His people?

3. Verse 6: What is God's ultimate purpose in saving sinners by grace?

4. Verse 11: What does this say about how God is working in the world?

5. Verses 13–14: What has God done for believers by the Holy Spirit?

6. Verses 17–19: What does Paul pray for believers?

7. Verses 20–21: What has God done for Christ? What difference does that make to Christians?

8. Verse 23: What is true of Christ's church?

DEVOTIONAL REFLECTIONS

1. The doctrine of election calls us to Christ. All of election's blessings are in Him. We dare not wait to come to Christ until we first somehow discover that we are elect. John Calvin said that the way to know that God elected us is by believing in Jesus Christ alone for salvation.

2. Election empowers holiness. Since God chose "that we should be holy" (v. 4), we must never isolate election from obeying God's laws. Those who say they can sin freely because they are elect have rejected the God who elects sinners unto holiness. Believers can pursue holiness confident that God's decree will give us all we need in Christ to attain it.

3. Grace fuels heartfelt praise. If your heart is sluggish in the aim for which we were made, it is the amazing grace of the triune God to sinners that you need most of all. Meditate on this chapter, and then make sure you take time to seek His face and sing His praises.

4. The gospel whets our appetite for God. Take Paul's prayer in this chapter and make it into your prayer for yourself and other believers. Stir up your heart with the glory of God's grace to desire to know Him better. Pray fervently for the Spirit of wisdom and revelation to give you more illumination about the riches of Jesus Christ.

Notes

1

2

3

4

5

6

7

8

Notes

9

10

11

12

13

14

15

Notes

16

17

18

19

20

21

22

STUDY QUESTIONS

1. Verse 1: What was our spiritual state before God saved us?

2. Verse 4: Why does God save sinners?

3. Verses 5–6: How does God save sinners?

4. Verses 8–10: What is the relationship between salvation and our works?

5. Verses 14–15: How has Christ reconciled Jews and Gentiles to each other and to God?

6. Verse 18: What role does each person in the Trinity have in our worship and prayers?

7. Verses 20–22: How are the people of the church like a temple?

DEVOTIONAL REFLECTIONS

1. The gospel demands humility. What reason do true Christians have to boast? We were dead in sin and distant from God. Satan ruled us, and God's wrath burned against us. If we have spiritual life, it is entirely due to God's grace in Christ. Why then do we look down on others? Who makes us to differ? Let us prostrate ourselves before the Lord Jesus, give all glory to God, and learn the meekness of the dove-like Spirit.

2. Believers are richer than kings. They are joined with none other than Jesus Christ, seated with Him in heavenly places. They are recreated with the risen Christ as their Adam. God will show how great He is by pouring out kindness upon them for all eternity. All of this is by grace through the great sufferings of Christ on the cross. If we are truly saved, we should bless God and sing His praises all our lives.

3. All nations are one at the foot of the cross. Despite our tendency to exalt ourselves and judge others based on race or culture, all believers are one and Christ is all. Let us therefore repent of our arrogance and welcome one another.

4. There is no sweeter place on earth than the gathered church. It is the temple of the living God, the dwelling place of His Spirit. Love the church. Serve the church. Stop complaining about the church. It is still under construction—as are its members.

Notes

1

2

3

4

5

6

7

Notes

8

9

10

11

12

13

14

15

16

Notes

17

18

19

20

21

STUDY QUESTIONS

1. Verses 3–5: How did God's apostles and prophets know His secret mystery?

2. Verse 6: What is the mystery that Paul proclaimed?

3. Verses 9–11: What does Paul say about God's purpose in Christ?

4. Verse 12: What do we have toward God by faith in Christ?

5. Verses 14–17: How is each person of the Trinity included in Paul's prayer?

6. Verse 19: What amazing request does Paul ask of God for the church?

7. Verses 20–21: What can give us confidence that God can and will do this?

DEVOTIONAL REFLECTIONS

1. Don't take the Bible or preaching for granted. It is an amazing gift of grace that God would reveal Christ to us. We never would have known the mystery of the gospel, but God has given it to us through the apostles and prophets so that His people might know His love. Furthermore, God's servants have suffered greatly through the ages to proclaim Christ's riches to the nations. Treasure the Word, read it often, and thank God for it.

2. In Christ believers have boldness and access with confidence to the Father. Do you experience that freedom in your prayers? The Father welcomes sinners into His presence with joy when they come in Jesus's name. God desires that His children pray with absolute confidence that He will be good to them (Luke 11:13).

3. Pray for great spiritual blessings for believers. God has given every blessing to us in the exalted Christ. The Spirit has already done a supernatural work of resurrection in everyone who now believes. Yet there is more of God's fullness for us to know. God is able to do far more than we can ask or imagine. John Newton said, "Thou art coming to a King; large petitions with thee bring; for His grace and power are such, none can ever ask too much." Begin by taking Paul's prayer in this chapter and praying it for your church.

Notes

1

2

3

4

5
6

7

8

9

10

Notes

11

12

13

14

15

16

Notes

17

18

19

20

21

22

23

24

Notes

25

26

27

28

29

30

31

32

1. Verses 1–3: What is a life "worthy" (or fitting) for the calling Christians have received?

2. Verses 4–6: How is Christian unity based on the Trinity and God's grace to us?

3. Verse 10: What is Christ's position at this present time? What is the purpose of His exaltation?

4. Verses 12–13: Why did Christ give to the church the ministers of the Word (v. 11)?

5. Verses 15–16: How can every member of the body contribute to its growth?

6. Verses 17–19: What is the spiritual condition of the Gentiles without Christ?

7. Verses 22–24: What are three basic duties of those in Christ?

8. Verse 25: What is an example of each of the three (vv. 22–24) with respect to our speech?

9. Verse 27: What might Christians do for the devil? How might they do that (v. 26)?

10. Verse 30: How should knowing that we have the Holy Spirit affect our lives?

11. Verse 32: How should the gospel shape how we treat one another?

DEVOTIONAL REFLECTIONS

1. Doctrine demands action, and a living faith produces works. It is presumptuous to rest in our knowledge about God if we do not walk in a manner fitting to that knowledge. Even the demons believe and tremble. The first response the gospel requires is humility. Those who believe the doctrines of grace should of all people be most humble. Therefore, let us examine ourselves, grieve over pride, pray for humility, and meditate on the gospel.

2. The life of the church revolves around Christ. Our unity springs from our union with God through Christ. Our abilities to serve flow from Christ's victory. Knowing Him and being like Him are our maturity and stability. He is the head from whom all members and relationships in the body draw life. Therefore, pray often for your church that Christ would be central in its worship and fellowship.

3. Repentance is fundamental to the Christian life. Turning from sin toward the Lord is the fundamental building block of faith. All Christians must continually put off sin and put on the image of Christ. Repentance is specific, and so the Bible's commandments address specific areas of life. Of the commands in this chapter, what is one area where you need to repent? What must you put off? Put on?

Notes

1

2

3

4

5

6

7

8

9

Notes

10

11

12

13

14

15

16

17

18

19

Notes

20

21

22

23

24

25

26

27

28

Notes

29

30

31

32

33

STUDY QUESTIONS

1. Verses 1–2: How should God's love for us in Christ change us?

2. Verses 5–6: What sober warning does Paul give here?

3. Verse 8: What were we formerly? What are we now if we are in Christ? What does this mean?

4. Verses 11–12: How should believers relate to the sins of this world?

5. Verse 16: How should believers treat their time? Why?

6. Verse 18: What responsibility do Christians have to the Holy Spirit? How is that the opposite of getting drunk?

7. Verses 19–21: What does the Holy Spirit produce in a church when He fills it?

8. Verse 23: Why should a woman submit to her husband?

9. Verses 25–27: How is Christ the ideal husband?

10. Verse 28: How should a man treat his wife? How would this shape his attitude toward her?

11. Verses 31–32: What Scripture passage does Paul quote? To whom does he apply it?

DEVOTIONAL REFLECTIONS

1. Christians must not be like the world. Too often the church wants to blend in, either to avoid persecution or to attract new members. But how can light blend into darkness without ceasing to be light? Our mission requires that we be different. The most effective outreach program produces people who radiate goodness, righteousness, and truth. Such Christians by their very lives convict sinners, validate God's law and judgment, and confirm the power of the gospel.

2. Pray for the Spirit to fill your church. Ask God to make your congregation a people who daily go to Christ and drink deeply of the intoxicating joy of the Holy Spirit. Seek the Spirit's grace for heartfelt singing of the psalms, profound thanksgiving to the Father through Christ, and humble submission to authority in the home, church, and state.

3. Marriage exists to show the glory of Christ. It is not a social contract formed when and how we please. It is not just a convenience for satisfying our desires. It is God's display case for the beautiful relationship between Christ and the church. Husbands and wives have a high calling. Commit yourself to serve your spouse as God commands in His Word—whether your marriage is sweet or sorrowful.

Notes

1

2

3

4

5

6

7

8

Notes

9

10

11

12

13

14

15

Notes

16

17

18

19

20

21

Notes

22

23

24

STUDY QUESTIONS

1. Verses 1–3: What commandment does Paul quote? How does he apply it?

2. Verse 4: What are the duties of a father to his children?

3. Verse 9: What must masters remember as they exercise authority over their servants?

4. Verse 12: Why must Christians need strength from the Lord (v. 10)?

5. Verses 14–17: What are the parts of the armor of God? How do we put them on?

6. Verse 18: What great Christian duty is foundational to our spiritual warfare?

7. Verses 21–22: How would the Ephesian saints know what was happening with Paul?

8. Verse 23: What does Paul pray for them in this benediction?

DEVOTIONAL REFLECTIONS

1. Paul's instructions for parenting are surprisingly simple. On the one hand, this is because the hardest thing about being a father or mother is doing what you know you should do: be kind and just, not angry and unfair; train and discipline your children consistently; teach them the Word of God. On the other hand, Paul's few words to fathers stand upon two broad bases. First, the book of Proverbs offers a wealth of wisdom for training children. Second, Ephesians 4–6 reminds us that successful parenting requires us to walk worthy of our calling in every area of life: church, daily repentance, avoiding worldliness, and marriages of love and respect. If we are faithful in these four areas, we have laid a solid foundation for raising our children.

2. No Christian is a spiritual civilian. We are all soldiers on the front lines. Therefore we must live in a state of battle-readiness, always alert for our enemy. Believers, however, need not live in bondage to fear. Christ is our armor, and He is sufficient to overcome a legion of fallen angels. Let us therefore make walking with Christ our lifestyle by meditating on the truth, doing what is right, resting on Christ's blood for peace of conscience, trusting God's promises, hoping in total salvation, speaking God's Word, and praying always for ourselves, other Christians, and the preachers of the gospel. By God's grace in Christ, we can overcome the Evil One.

Introduction to the Book of
PHILIPPIANS

AUTHORSHIP: Paul wrote the epistle to the Philippians (1:1). The apostle ministered to the church in Philippi and was familiar with the believers there (Acts 16:12; 20:1–6). The epistle contains many personal references to the apostle, such as his stay in prison (Phil. 1:12–26), his personal interaction with Epaphroditus (2:25–30), and his personal testimony (3:4–7). The apostle's authorship is beyond doubt and has not been seriously questioned from the early church to the present day.

DATE: The date of Paul's epistle depends on which imprisonment he was enduring while he wrote Philippians. There are three main views: Ephesus, Caesarea, and Rome. Given that there is no definitive evidence supporting Paul's being imprisoned in Ephesus this view is the least likely. He was in prison in Caesarea (AD 57–59), but Paul's comments about the palace (1:13) and his statement about the possibility of impending death (vv. 20–26) do not seem to fit as well with Caesarea as they do with Rome. The traditional view sees Paul writing to the believers in Philippi during the latter end of his Roman imprisonment around AD 61 or 62.

THEME: Paul writes to encourage the believers to joyfully persevere in the gospel in spite of present difficulties and trying circumstances, expressing confidence that the God who began a good work in them will complete it (1:6).

PURPOSE: To encourage faithful believers and spur them on to further humility, unity, joy, and peace by an undistracted pursuit of Christ and His likeness.

SYNOPSIS

The Contribution of Philippians to Redemptive Revelation
Epaphroditus's return to Philippi occasioned the writing of Philippians as Paul corresponded with the Christians in Philippi through him (2:25). Throughout the letter, Paul expresses his love for them and his continued prayers on their behalf (1:3–8; 4:10). As Paul wrote, he was

imprisoned and wrote to inform the Philippians of his present situation, that his chains have been for the advancement of the gospel (1:12–18). In light of the sufferings that God ordains for His church (v. 29), Paul encourages the church to Christlike unity and humility (1:27–2:18) and warns of the false teachers who threaten the purity of the gospel by calling the Philippians to return to Judaism (3:1–21).

Paul highly commended this faithful church, and called them to make it their highest ambition to know Christ better and be more like Him, for He is our joy and peace. Several themes contribute to this great river of blessedness. First, Paul assures them of his love for them and his continued prayers to God on their behalf (1:3–8). Second, he writes to them concerning his present situation in prison. He reminds those who possibly misunderstood his choices that led to his imprisonment that what has taken place has been for the advancement of the gospel (vv. 12–18). Third, Paul encourages the church to strive for unity and harmony in the midst of their own difficulties and trials, pointing them to the ultimate example of humility and selflessness, Jesus Christ (1:27–2:18). Fourth, Paul warns the church of false teachers who threaten the purity of the gospel by returning to Judaism, exhorting the believers to continue pursuing Christ and following the pattern set by the apostle himself (3:1–21). Fifth, Paul expresses thanks to the church for their gift to him (4:10) and exhorts them to receive Epaphroditus with gladness and to hold him in high regard (2:25–30).

Philippians reminds Christians that though they often find themselves in difficult circumstances, this should not make them call God's love and care into question. Rather, trials are used to further the witness of the gospel and to mature Christians in their faith and sanctification. Paul reminds the Philippian believers that God has not only given the gift of faith but also the gift of suffering for His sake (1:29). Paul applies this to his own circumstances in prison and to the circumstances of the believers to whom he is writing. Even though trials often tempt believers to become divided, Paul encourages them to embrace suffering and give themselves to selfless, Christlike living. While life on the timeline between the work of grace begun and the work of grace completed is often hard, Paul expresses confidence that God's grace will sustain them (v. 6). Paul also encourages believers that regardless of life's difficulties, joy ought to characterize Christians. Neither joy nor contentment are rooted in circumstances, either good or bad, but in Jesus Christ. In order to lead Christians to greater Christlikeness, Paul pens one of the most beautiful statements of Christology (2:6–11). If Christ, who is God, joyfully and humbly took on humanity to give Himself in death for others, then we, too, can esteem others better than ourselves as we press on toward the mark of the high calling of God in Christ Jesus.

OUTLINE

I. Introduction (1:1–11)

II. Paul's Rejoicing in Present Circumstances (1:12–26)
    A. Gospel Advancement through Imprisonment (1:12–13)
    B. Gospel Advancement through Preaching Christ (1:14–18)
    C. Living and Dying Is Viewed as Gaining Christ (1:19–26)

III. Paul's Exhortations to the Church (1:27–2:18)
    A. Live a Life Consistent with the Gospel of Christ (1:27–30)
    B. Live in Humble, Selfless Unity with the Body of Christ (2:1–11)
    C. Live as Lights in a Dark World (2:12–18)

IV. Paul's Report Concerning Timothy and Epaphroditus (2:19–30)

V. Paul's Warnings (3:1–21)
    A. Paul's Warning against Judaizers (3:1–11)
    B. Paul's Personal Testimony of Advancing in the Gospel (3:12–16)
    C. Paul's Warning against Lawlessness (3:17–21)

VI. Paul's Concluding Exhortations and Thanksgiving (4:1–23)

Notes

1

2

3

4

5

6

7

8

9

Notes

10

11

12

13

14

15

16

Notes

17

18

19

20

21

22

23

Notes

24

25

26

27

28

29

30

STUDY QUESTIONS

1. Verse 1: To whom did Paul address this letter? To whom does each of these terms refer?

2. Verse 6: What confidence can a believer have about the future?

3. Verses 9–11: What did Paul pray for the saints in Philippi?

4. Verse 12: Why could Paul rejoice, though he was imprisoned?

5. Verse 15: What motives might move a person to preach the gospel of Christ?

6. Verses 19–20: What was Paul's positive expectation about his own future?

7. Verse 21: What was Paul's perspective on life and death? What does this mean?

8. Verse 23: Why is death even better than life for the believer?

9. Verse 27: What kind of conduct is fitting for believers in the gospel?

10. Verse 29: What has the Lord granted to His people?

DEVOTIONAL REFLECTIONS

1. It is easy to enter the place of prayer mindlessly, falling prey to vain repetitions. Sometimes we struggle with knowing what to pray for or how to shape our prayers. Paul's prayer in the opening section of this chapter models for us a biblically informed prayer. Prayer is to be a part of the regular rhythm of a Christian's life. Prayer expresses itself in thanksgiving to God and in intercession for others. Paul does not merely make general requests of blessing, but specifically prays that God would work in Christians' lives and grow them in love for the purpose of knowing how to live in this world.

2. What do you live for? Is the fame of Christ's name more important to you, or is comfort and ease of life? Paul's life was so wrapped up in Christ and the gospel that he wanted nothing more than to see the gospel advance, even if it meant that others sought to add to his affliction. When life's circumstances get difficult, it is easy to become focused on self and how to minimize discomfort. But Paul encourages us to remain firm and live in a way that is worthy of the gospel.

Notes

1

2

3

4

5

6

7

8

9

10

11

12

13

14

15

Notes

16

17

18

19

20

21

22

23

24

Notes

25

26

27

28

29

30

STUDY QUESTIONS

1. Verse 3: What should never be our motivation?
   What should it be?

2. Verse 5: What great example should we imitate in our mindset?

3. Verses 6–8: Who is the ultimate model of humbling oneself?
   How so?

4. Verses 9–11: How did God the Father respond to Christ's humbling
   Himself?

5. Verses 12–13: What is our duty? How is this done entirely by
   God's grace?

6. Verses 19–22: How is Timothy (KJV, Timotheus) an example of
   Christlikeness?

7. Verse 25: How does Paul describe Epaphroditus?

8. Verses 26–27: What happened to Epaphroditus? How was his
   situation remedied?

9. Verses 29–30: Why should the church honor people like
   Epaphroditus?

DEVOTIONAL REFLECTIONS

1. Meditate on the wonder of the incarnation of the Son of God. Consider the humiliation of Christ in His birth, life, and death. Praise God
the Father for the gift of the Son, who willingly submitted Himself to
die the shameful death of the cross to redeem unworthy sinners.

2. Christ deserves our all. Consider the commands in verses 3–5, 12–16
and think practically about what they call you to. How did Timothy
(vv. 19–24) and Epaphroditus (vv. 25–30) model obedience to these
commands?

Notes

1

2

3

4

5

6

7

Notes

8

9

10

11

12

13

Notes

14

15

16

17

18

19

20

Notes

21

STUDY QUESTIONS

1. Verse 3: Who are "the circumcision"—that is, the true covenant people of God?

2. Verses 5–6: How could Paul have put confidence in himself for his righteousness?

3. Verses 8–9: What is the value of knowing Christ? What can we find in Christ alone?

4. Verse 12: What was Paul's attitude and ambition regarding his own spiritual progress?

5. Verse 15: What did Paul expect God would do for believers who did not share his mindset?

6. Verses 18–19: How did Paul describe many who are enemies of Christ's cross?

7. Verses 20–21: What is the Christian's citizenship (KJV, conversation)? What will Christ do for believers when He comes from heaven?

DEVOTIONAL REFLECTIONS

1. In what ways are you tempted to boast in your accomplishments? Are you actively pursuing an experiential knowledge of Christ? The Christian life is one of growth. Paul uses the language of a race (v. 14) and he highlights the importance of constantly making Christ the prize after which he runs.

2. Paul reminds believers that their citizenship is in heaven, where Jesus Christ is and where we are to look. He tells them that when Jesus Christ arrives they will be changed into their glorified bodies. That happens in an instant. If seeing Christ physically changes you in a moment, then you should recognize that seeing Christ now spiritually changes you progressively. This is progressive sanctification. How do you seek to daily gaze on Christ and lead others to do the same?

Notes

1

2

3

4

5

6

7

Notes

8

9

10

11

12

13

14

Notes

15

16

17

18

19

20

21

22

23

STUDY QUESTIONS

1. Verse 1: What did Paul say about the saints in Philippi?

2. Verse 4: What command did Paul give—twice—to believers? How (vv. 5–13)?

3. Verse 8: On what things should believers set their minds?

4. Verses 11–13: What had Paul learned? How is that possible?

5. Verses 15–16: What was special about the church in Philippi?

6. Verse 18: How is a financial gift to a missionary an offering to God?

7. Verse 19: What promise does Paul give to this generous church?

8. Verse 20: How do the things taught in this chapter lead to the glory of God forever?

DEVOTIONAL REFLECTIONS

1. How do you handle the concerns of life? Is prayer to God a first or last option? Paul, like Peter, encourages us to cast all those things that cause anxiety upon the Lord in prayer. What is true about God that encourages believers to pray? Why should we add thanksgiving to our supplications?

2. Contentment is a battle. It is easy to think that we will achieve it if only our circumstances change. Yet, Paul says that he had to learn contentment even when he was abounding. Jesus Christ is the prize of the believer. All things, either poverty or prosperity, cannot compare to knowing and having Christ. Extol Christ in your life and in your home in a manner that clearly demonstrates He is the key to contentment.

Introduction to the Book of
COLOSSIANS

AUTHORSHIP: The apostle Paul identifies himself as the author, along with Timothy, who possibly served as his scribe in writing (1:1). The letter contains a first person reference in v. 23 and closes with the words, "The salutation by the hand of me Paul" (4:18). While some scholars have cast doubt on Pauline authorship because of stylistic and theological differences, their arguments are not convincing. While some of the style and language are specific to the Colossian situation, there is much in the letter that fits Paul's other writings. Regarding the theology of the book, while the specifics of the threat of a worldly "philosophy" (2:8) are unique to the church in Colosse, Paul's emphasis on a high Christology and the centrality of the gospel to combat such a threat is in keeping with the theology of Paul's other letters. There is little reason to doubt the authenticity of Pauline authorship.

Colossians is considered one of the Prison Epistles (4:3, 18) and it is believed that Paul wrote this while imprisoned in Rome. This fits with Paul's references to Aristarchus and Luke (4:10, 14; see also Acts 27:2).

DATE: Paul wrote the letter from prison in Rome around AD 61 or 62.

THEME: The supremacy of Christ over all things.

PURPOSE: To ground and settle the Colossians in the knowledge of Christ against error.

SYNOPSIS
The Contribution of Colossians to Redemptive Revelation
Though Paul did not plant the church in Colosse or visit the believers there, he cared deeply for the church and received reports regarding the church's health. Upon hearing that false teachers threatened the purity of the gospel of free grace, Paul responded with a letter. Though there are certainly difficulties in grasping a full understanding of the threat the Colossian believers faced, it is clear that it demanded adherence to external rites, that it was according to men and contrary to Christ (2:8, 20–21). Paul responds by reminding the church that

Jesus Christ is supreme over all creation and over the new creation (the church). Therefore, anything that detracts from the supremacy of Christ is to be repudiated. Paul intercedes for them and encourages them, that rather than becoming pulled away from the faith that they learned from Epaphras (1:7), they will continue to grow in and be filled with the knowledge of God's will in all wisdom and spiritual understanding (v. 9).

The Christian life becomes visible in everyday life; it is distinct from the world. There must be a change in the heart, though, before there is change in one's life. The Colossian believers faced a teaching that following certain external rules would make a person more spiritual (2:21). This teaching was contrary to the gospel of Christ and resulted in a form of religion that, while it may have appeared to be wise and humble (v. 23), actually threatened the sufficiency of the gospel. Because of this threat, Paul wrote to the Colossians to encourage them to continue in the faith of Christ that they initially received (v. 6). Instead of following after man-made wisdom, believers should continue to pursue Christ, in whom are hid all the treasures of wisdom and knowledge (v. 3).

Therefore, the greatest antidote to external religion is a clearer vision of the person and work of Jesus Christ (1:15–22). Seeing Christ, in whom the fullness of the Godhead dwells bodily (v. 19; 2:9), is utterly transforming. Paul highlights this in his prayer and works it out in greater detail in chapters 2–3. Knowing God's will, grasping one's union with Christ in His death and resurrection, and fixing one's mind on things above where Christ is leads to Christlikeness, which is the goal of sanctification (3:10). Because Christ is sufficient for both justification and sanctification, the Christian should not shortchange himself by conforming merely to external forms of religion. All that he has and needs is found in Christ. Paul is quick to remind them that relying solely on Christ and living in light of the resurrection does not lead to licentiousness. Rather, those in Christ, as the elect of God, are holy and live holy lives (3:12–4:1). Reading Colossians and grasping its message brings the believer into a deeper and greater experience of the blessings found in Jesus Christ, the visible image of the invisible God.

OUTLINE

I. Introduction (1:1–14)
   A. Greetings (1:1–2)
   B. Thanksgiving (1:3–8)
   C. Prayer (1:9–14)

II. Glorying in the Supremacy of Christ (1:15–23)
   A. Supremacy of Christ over Creation (1:15–17)
   B. Supremacy of Christ over the New Creation (1:18)
   C. Supremacy of Christ in the Work of Redemption (1:19–23)

III. Paul's Ministry and Conflict for the Colossian Believers (1:24–2:7)
   A. Paul's Ministry of Preaching the Mystery of God(1:24–29)
   B. Paul's Concern for the Colossian Believers (2:1–7)

IV. Paul's Warning of and Solution to False Teaching (2:8–23)
   A. Summary of False Teaching (2:8)
   B. Sufficiency of Christ's Death and Resurrection (2:9–15)
   C. False Teaching Described in Greater Detail (2:16–23)

V. Paul's Description of the Christian Life (3:1–4:6)
   A. Foundation of the Christian Life Wrapped Up in Christ (3:1–4)
   B. The Mortification of Sin (3:5–11)
   C. The Putting On of Holiness (3:12–17)
   D. Description of the Christian Life in the Household (3:18–4:1)
   E. The Christian's Prayer Life (4:2–4)
   F. The Christian's Life before the World (4:5–6)

VI. Final Words (4:7–18)
   A. Comments regarding Paul's Companions (4:7–14)
   B. Final Greetings to the Brethren and the Benediction (4:15–18)

Notes

1

2

3

4

5

6

7

Notes

8

9

10

11

12

13

14

15

Notes

16

17

18

19

20

21

22

Notes

23

24

25

26

27

Notes

28

29

1. Verses 3–6: For what does Paul thank God regarding the Colossian saints?

2. Verse 9: What does Paul pray for them? What does that imply about spiritual growth?

3. Verses 10–12: What are four parts of walking in a manner worthy of the Lord?

4. Verses 13–14: How does Paul describe salvation?

5. Verse 16: What did the Father do "by" and "for" His Son? What does that imply about Christ?

6. Verse 18: What was the purpose of Christ being the "firstborn from the dead"?

7. Verse 21: What was our spiritual state before God reconciled us to Himself?

8. Verse 23: What must we do if we will fully and finally be saved?

9. Verse 27: What is the believer's hope of glory? Why (Col. 3:4)?

10. Verses 28–29: What characterized Paul's ministry? How is he a model for ministers?

DEVOTIONAL REFLECTIONS

1. Give attention to the great wonder of the incarnation. Meditate upon the supremacy of Christ in His person as the agent, sustainer, and goal of creation, considering that this person would take on flesh to redeem you from your sins. What are some reasons why Christ's incarnation would make you praise God?

2. Paul prays that the believers at Colosse might be filled with the knowledge of God. He prays that they might "walk worthy of the Lord unto all pleasing" (v. 10). Believers tend to think of God's will as that which only deals with future plans. Yet Paul writes about God's will as informing our lives in the present and how we may live before God, being fruitful in every good work.

Notes

1

2

3

4

5

6

7

Notes

8

9

10

11

12

13

Notes

14

15

16

17

18

19

Notes

20

21

22

23

STUDY QUESTIONS

1. Verse 3: Where has God placed all the treasures of His wisdom and knowledge for us?

2. Verses 6–7: How should believers walk in Christ?

3. Verses 9–10: What is it about Christ that makes Him fully sufficient for us and supreme over all powers?

4. Verses 14–15: What two things against us did Christ overcome at the cross?

5. Verses 16–17: What requirements no longer bind believers? Why?

6. Verse 19: What is the fundamental mistake of false teachers?

7. Verses 21–22: What kind of commandments and doctrines were these teachers advocating?

8. Verse 23: What forms of false spirituality do we find here?

DEVOTIONAL REFLECTIONS

1. In Christ are all the treasures of wisdom and knowledge. Yet, we so often seek guidance for life outside of Christ. Whether it be self-help tips or the latest marketing fad, we can be tempted to find quick solutions to life's problems outside of Christ. Give yourself, by grace, to a perpetual pursuit of experiencing Christ and living in the enjoyment of being united to Him.

2. How ought you to view your standards of conduct? When Paul says that external things do not conquer the indulgences of the flesh, is he advocating the repudiation of all standards? Consider the sufficiency of Christ's death and resurrection to sanctify, along with the motivation of the standards set forth, personally and for family.

Notes

1

2

3

4

5

6

7

8

9

Notes

10

11

12

13

14

15

16

Notes

17

18

19

20

21

22

23

24

25

STUDY QUESTIONS

1. Verses 1–2: Where should a Christian's thoughts and desires be focused?

2. Verse 4: What does this teach about Christ? About the future of believers?

3. Verses 8–9: What are some attitudes and actions that believers must put off?

4. Verses 12–14: What affections and conduct must believers put on?

5. Verse 16: How does this verse compare to Ephesians 5:18–19? What might that imply?

6. Verse 19: What should husbands avoid in their attitude and dealings with their wives?

7. Verses 22–25: What do these instructions to servants say to us all about our work?

DEVOTIONAL REFLECTIONS

1. Believers are risen with Christ and exhorted to fix their minds on things above. Do you give attention to this focus in your personal walk and in your family? Do you find strength (1:11) to mortify and put off sin in God's power? Perhaps you are frustrated seeking to mortify sin in your own strength. What does living according to 3:12–16 look like in your personal interactions and in your family life?

2. Notice the manifold grace of the Holy Spirit (vv. 12–15) with which we are commanded to clothe ourselves. Reflect practically on what this calls you to do or perhaps change in your life.

3. Talk through the responsibilities of husband, wife, father, mother, and children with the whole family present (vv. 18–25). Consider that each relationship is lived under God, before whom all relationships are accountable.

Notes

1

2

3

4

5

6

7

8

Notes

9

10

11

12

13

14

15

Notes

16

17

18

STUDY QUESTIONS

1. Verses 2–4: What does Paul teach us about prayer?

2. Verses 5–6: What does Paul teach us about how we should act and talk with unbelievers?

3. Verse 9: How does Paul describe Onesimus? Who was he (Philemon 10–21)?

4. Verses 12–13: How is Epaphras an example of a godly minister?

5. Verse 16: What were the churches to do with Paul's epistles? How do we do that today?

6. Verse 17: What was Paul's exhortation to Archippus? What would that require him to do?

DEVOTIONAL REFLECTIONS

1. Prayer is vital for the Christian life. Prayer ought to be thoughtful. It involves thanksgiving and intercession. It is easy to neglect thanksgiving, but believers have so much for which they ought to praise God. Believers ought also to remember to intercede for others, especially as it relates to the advancement of the gospel. Teach your family to pray regularly, thoughtfully, thankfully, and missionally.

2. What does it mean to make your speech around unbelievers "seasoned with salt" (v. 6)? What unbelievers do you talk to? How can you bring grace and salt into your conversations with them?

Introduction to the Book of
1 THESSALONIANS

AUTHORSHIP: Paul's authorship of 1 Thessalonians was widely accepted in the early church. Church fathers such as Irenaeus (c. AD 130–200), Clement of Alexandria (c. AD 150–215), and Tertullian (c. AD 160–225) all acknowledged Pauline authorship of 1 Thessalonians. Until the mid-nineteenth century, Pauline authorship was almost unanimously agreed upon. Thessalonica was an important port city in Macedonia and was situated along the *Via Egnatia*, which served as the main Roman road near Asia Minor. Greeks, Romans, and Jews all lived in Thessalonica and idolatry ran rampant throughout the city. Paul had brought the gospel to the people of Thessalonica while on his second missionary journey, along with Silas and Timothy, his missionary colleagues. The events connected with this missionary outreach to Thessalonica are recorded in Acts 17:1–10. At Thessalonica Paul had preached first to the Jews. But they had rejected Paul's evidence to show that Jesus is their Messiah. Wonderfully, however, a large number of Greeks had come to saving faith in Christ. But persecution and civil disturbance had resulted and the Christian converts sent Paul and Silas away by night for their safety. The missionaries then came to Berea, where young Timothy joined them. Now, understandably, Paul was concerned for the converts in Thessalonica. But Timothy was able to report to him that these converts were standing fast in the faith.

DATE: It is commonly believed that Paul wrote 1 Thessalonians after Timothy arrived in Corinth, where Paul spent a number of months (AD 51–52). It is likely that Paul wrote this epistle around AD 52.

THEME: Endure suffering.

PURPOSE: To encourage believers with the hope of Christ's return.

SYNOPSIS
The Contribution of 1 Thessalonians to Redemptive Revelation
This epistle is written to make clear to the young church at Thessalonica, Paul's affectionate and heartfelt concern for their spiritual and

moral well-being. In the course of his address to them he gives them assurance of their "election of God" (1:4), his appreciation of their evangelistic zeal (v. 8), his gratitude that many have received the gospel as from God (2:13), and many tokens of his love and prayerful concern (3:9–10). In the course of his letter he takes care to vindicate his own motives as a genuine servant of God (2:1–10) and he explains the sad state of the Jewish nation on that date, since they were exposed to the message of the gospel (vv. 14–16). Two clear notes which he weaves into his epistle also are: (1) the great importance to the believer of holiness (4:1–8); and (2) the need to watch and pray so that we may not be "asleep" when our blessed Savior comes to judge the whole world in righteousness (5:1–8). The epistle is notable for the numerous basic exhortations with which it ends (v. 16–22).

This epistle reflects the joy and relief of Paul upon hearing that the Thessalonian believers were standing firm: "For now we live, if ye stand fast in the Lord" (3:8). The apostle does not give detailed theological teaching in this letter, although he does give comforting instruction on the state of believers after death, and of the happiness awaiting believers at the second coming of Christ (4:13–18).

OUTLINE
I. Greetings (1:1)

II. Paul's Response to the Good Report Concerning the Thessalonians (1:2–3:13)
    A. Grounds for Believing the Faith of His Readers Is Genuine (1:2–10)
    B. Paul's Tenderness, Affection, Sincerity, and Propriety toward Them (2:1–13)
    C. The Sad Condition of the Persecutors (2:14–16)
    D. Paul's Comfort Because They Were Steadfast in Their Faith (2:17–3:10)
    E. Paul's Affectionate Prayer for Them and His Wish to See Them Soon (3:11–13)

III. Paul's Exhortations to the Thessalonian Believers (4:1–5:28)
    A. The Need for Christians to Be Holy (4:1–12)
    B. The Second Coming of Christ (4:13–5:11)
    C. Various Exhortations (5:12–22)
    D. Closing Prayer, Greeting, and Benediction (5:23–28)

Notes

1

2

3

4

5

6

7

Notes

8

9

10

STUDY QUESTIONS

1. Verse 1: From whom do grace and peace come? What does this reveal about Christ?

2. Verses 4–6: How did Paul know that God had elected (or chosen) these people?

3. Verse 9: What does this teach us about true conversion?

4. Verse 10: What does this verse say about the Christian hope?

DEVOTIONAL REFLECTIONS

1. When we understand the Bible's teachings aright, we see that coming by faith to Christ could never happen as a result of our own free will. True faith is God-given and therefore, if we are believers, we should thank God that He has given us the ability to come to Jesus and to believe in Him, as Paul here shows (v. 4).

2. It cannot be too strongly noted that the only evidence of a person's being one of God's elect is when they live a godly life and so bring forth the fruits of righteousness. Election makes men saints, not mere religious talkers, learned hypocrites, or adherents to some religious group.

Notes

1

2

3

4

5

6

7

8

Notes

9

10

11

12

13

14

Notes

15

16

17

18

19

20

STUDY QUESTIONS

1. Verses 3–6: What do faithful gospel preachers avoid in their ministry?

2. Verses 7–8: How are ministers like mothers?

3. Verses 9–12: How are ministers like fathers?

4. Verse 13: What does this teach about the word preached by the apostles?

5. Verse 14: How did the converts in Thessalonica become like the saints in Judea?

6. Verse 18: Who hindered Paul from returning to them? How might he have done that?

7. Verses 19–20: What did Paul say that these saints would be at the coming of Christ?

DEVOTIONAL REFLECTIONS

1. Contrary to what we often think, affliction produces greater confidence and boldness in the people of God (v. 2). If it is viewed rightly, affliction takes our confidence away from ourselves and other people, and settles it on the gospel and God alone.

2. Tenderness for the Lord's people is one of the characteristics of a spiritual preacher. Paul uses the pictures of a nurse (v. 7) and a father (v. 11). How do both kinds of love form a good soil for spiritual growth?

Notes

1

2

3

4

5

6

Notes

7

8

9

10

11

12

13

STUDY QUESTIONS

1. Verse 3: To what has God appointed His people?

2. Verse 7: What comforted Paul and his fellow missionaries?

3. Verse 10: Why did Paul desire to visit the Thessalonian church again?

4. Verses 12–13: What did Paul pray for them?

DEVOTIONAL REFLECTIONS

1. People in the pew do not always understand how great a burden their ministers carry day and night for their eternal good. Spend a little time praying for your ministers and elders that God would give them patience, endurance, and wisdom in shepherding the flock of Christ.

2. It is an encouraging thing for Christians to meditate on the return of Christ and the grace and glory He will usher in. Believers must always have one eye on the great day when our Lord will return and His people will be eternally at peace. At the same time, we must not forget that we live in this world and thus must await the return of Christ.

Notes

1

2

3

4

5

6

7

Notes

8

9

10

11

12

13

14

Notes

15

16

17

18

STUDY QUESTIONS

1. Verse 1: What does Paul exhort these believers to do?

2. Verse 3: What is the will of God for His church?

3. Verses 6–8: What motives does Paul give to believers to avoid sexual immorality?

4. Verses 9–10: Why do the saints already love each other? What is their duty now?

5. Verses 16–17: What is the hope of believers in Christ?

6. Verse 18: How should we make practical use of this truth? How might you do that?

DEVOTIONAL REFLECTIONS

1. Sanctification involves careful obedience to the Ten Commandments, a number of which are addressed in this chapter. When we are saved by grace, we do not leave behind the commandments of God. On the contrary, we find the power to keep them in love.

2. Believers sorrow when their Christian brothers and sisters die, but their sorrow is mingled with comfort to know they shall soon be with them again forever, when Christ returns. When you think about the deaths of your loved ones, keep one eye on Christ's coming, and you will find comfort.

Notes

1

2

3

4

5

6

7

8

Notes

9

10

11

12

13

14

15

16

17

Notes

18

19
20
21

22
23

24

25
26

27

28

STUDY QUESTIONS

1. Verses 2–3: How will the day of the Lord come on the wicked?

2. Verse 6: How should believers be different from the wicked?

3. Verse 9: Why can believers in Christ anticipate the day of the Lord with confidence?

4. Verses 12–13: How should the saints treat the officers of the church?

5. Verse 14: How do different kinds of people require different kinds of ministry?

6. Verses 16–18: What is always God's will for us? Why is each of these important?

7. Verse 21: What is required of believers here (note the context, v. 20)?

8. Verses 23–24: What does Paul pray for the saints? Why is he confident in the answer?

9. Verse 27: What did Paul require the church to do with his letter?

DEVOTIONAL REFLECTIONS

1. Believers have the sure and blessed hope of heaven forever. Therefore, seek by God's grace to live for the glory of our great Lord and Savior. Do not be seduced by the glitter and glamour of this world, for God will take it away in a moment.

2. The unconverted are like men who are asleep on an express train soon to plunge into an ocean of fire and misery. Should they not be warned and told of the God who sent His Son to die for lost sinners? Let us speak the gospel to our family and neighbors and support the gospel preaching of our ministers and missionaries with encouragement, prayer, and financial gifts.

3. God is in this life sanctifying His people through His Word of truth. Therefore let us be those who value the Bible as our greatest earthly treasure.

Introduction to the Book of
2 THESSALONIANS

AUTHORSHIP: The author of this epistle identifies himself as Paul (1:1; 3:17). The early church and biblical scholarship throughout most of history have held to its Pauline authorship. Some modern scholars have argued that 1 and 2 Thessalonians present different theological perspectives on the end times, and therefore Paul wrote the first but not the second epistle. Some scholars also identify the "man of sin" (2:3) with the legend of the return of Nero from the dead (*Nero redivivus*), which arose after Paul had died. Neither of these arguments warrants the conclusion that Paul is not the author. First, the teachings of both epistles on the coming of Christ are quite compatible. Second, the idea of an antichrist goes back at least to the prophet Daniel (Dan. 11:36). It would be remarkably hypocritical for the author to write severely against deception and lies (2 Thess. 2:3, 9–12) and to commend "the love of the truth" (v. 10) if he were presenting himself under a false name. The best reading of the epistle is that it was written by "Paul," the apostle closely associated with Silvanus (or Silas) and Timotheus (or Timothy) (1:1; Acts 15:40; 16:1–3; 2 Cor. 1:1, 19)—the same three persons mentioned in the opening of 1 Thessalonians.

DATE: Though a few scholars have argued that 2 Thessalonians came before what we call 1 Thessalonians, they have no definitive proof. Paul writes of an "epistle" he previously sent to this church (2:15), which most likely refers to 1 Thessalonians. It appears that 2 Thessalonians was written several months after 1 Thessalonians (see Introduction to 1 Thessalonians), during Paul's second missionary journey. He probably wrote from Corinth where Silas and Timothy had joined him (Acts 18:1, 5).

THEME: The coming judgment against those who persecute the glorious saints of Christ.

PURPOSE: To balance the expectations in the church about the end times, revealing that Christ's coming has not yet happened, but when it does, He will come with judgment and glory.

SYNOPSIS

The Contribution of 2 Thessalonians to Redemptive Revelation

This is a short epistle but it contains very important teaching, both theological and practical. Its burden is to correct a misunderstanding that had evidently been reported to Paul as having harmfully influenced the faith of the Thessalonian believers. The error Paul corrects is the mistaken idea that Christ's second coming was just moments away (2:1). Before Christ returns, he says, there must be revealed a notable enemy of God on the stage of history called "that man of sin" (v. 3). Evidently some of the church members at Thessalonica had been so influenced by the expectation of an immediate coming of Christ that they were not working to support themselves and their families. Paul denounces this as utterly immoral. He lays down the healthy principle that if any do not work, neither should they eat (3:10). If a church member does not work, he is choosing to starve. Then he should be judged "disorderly" (v. 11). Such persons should be made to feel "ashamed" (v. 14).

OUTLINE

I.   Salutation: Grace and Peace (1:1–2)

II. Courage for Suffering Saints (1:3–12)
   A. Thanksgiving for Faith, Love, and Endurance (1:3–4)
   B. Judgment on Persecutors and Glory for Saints (1:5–10)
   C. Prayer for Power and Glory (1:11–12)

III. Correction of Mistaken End-Times Expectations (2:1–12)
   A. The False Report of the Day of Christ (2:1–2)
   B. The Rise and Destruction of the Man of Sin (2:3–12)

IV. Confidence in Salvation and Call to Prayer (2:13–3:5)
   A. Thanksgiving and Exhortation to Elect Saints (2:13–15)
   B. Prayer for Comfort and Strength (2:16–17)
   C. Request for Prayer for the Mission (3:1–2)
   D. Assurance and Prayer for Endurance (3:3–5)
   E. Command to Discipline Disorderly Brothers (3:6–15)

V. Farewell: Peace and Grace (3:16–18)

Notes

1

2

3

4

5

6

Notes

7

8

9

10

11

12

STUDY QUESTIONS

1. Verse 3: Why did Paul thank God for the church in Thessalonica?

2. Verses 4–5: What was a sign that these believers would inherit the kingdom of God?

3. Verses 7–9: What will Christ do to unbelievers when He comes again?

4. Verses 11–12: What was Paul's prayer for this church?

DEVOTIONAL REFLECTIONS

1. The best Christians are sometimes those who are suffering the worst persecution. We should pray daily for our brothers and sisters in lands that are hostile to the gospel. Use missionary newsletters, websites, maps, and other tools to pray intelligently for the persecuted church.

2. We are not to avenge ourselves on those who do us harm, but we are ever to keep in mind the truth that God will take vengeance on those who do us any injury because of our faith. This is the key to freedom from bitterness: trusting that God's justice will prevail. How have you suffered for Christ? How does this truth help you?

3. It is not a kindness in our preaching to the unconverted to keep from them the fearful reality of hell, with its "flaming fire" (v. 8) and its "everlasting destruction" (v. 9). Pray for preachers that they would boldly preach both law and gospel, both hell and heaven.

Notes

1

2

3

4

5

6

7

Notes

8

9

10

11

12

13

Notes

14

15

16

17

STUDY QUESTIONS

1. Verses 1–3: What must take place before the coming of Christ?

2. Verse 4: What will the "man of sin" (or "lawlessness") do?

3. Verse 8: What will bring this evil man's work to an end?

4. Verses 10–12: Why will God give people over to believe this delusion?

5. Verses 13–14: Why do some people believe in Christ instead of Satan's lies?

6. Verses 16–17: What does Paul pray for the church?

DEVOTIONAL REFLECTIONS

1. Gregory the Great (d. AD 604) said that anyone who claims to be the Universal Priest over all the church is the precursor of the Antichrist. Many Christians, including John Wycliffe, Martin Luther, John Calvin, and the authors of the Westminster Confession of Faith, have understood the "man of sin" to be the Pope of Rome. Other Christians expect a future Antichrist to arise. However we interpret this text, we must certainly reject anyone who seeks to take a place of authority in the church that belongs only to the Lord. Christ alone has supreme authority to teach the church its doctrines, laws, and worship. Christ alone is the Mediator who atones for sin by His once-for-all sacrifice. Christ alone has the power of the Spirit to make the means of grace effective to save sinners. Take no part in a church that makes a man into Christ's substitute. Is there anyone or anything that is distracting you from Christ?

2. The only alternative to being swept up in the worship of men is salvation by the sovereign grace of God. Wherever we see people exercising faith in Christ and practical holiness, let us give thanks to God for choosing and calling them to Christ. If God has saved you, thank Him every day. If you cannot say that you know you belong to Christ, do not keep rejecting the love of the truth, or God could give you over to delusion. Turn from your sins and cry out in prayer to Christ even now to save you.

Notes

1

2

3

4

5

6

7

Notes

8

9

10

11

12

13

14

Notes

15

16

17

18

STUDY QUESTIONS

1. Verses 1–2: What does Paul ask the church to pray for his missionary team?

2. Verse 6: What should the church do with brothers or sisters engaged in disorderly conduct?

3. Verse 10: What general rule did Paul give them? What does this mean?

4. Verse 12: What should be the practice of Christians, insofar as they are able?

5. Verses 14–15: How should the church treat Christians who disobey this rule? Where does this fit in the overall process of church discipline (Matt. 18:15–17)?

6. Verse 17: How did Paul authenticate that his letters came from him?

DEVOTIONAL REFLECTIONS

1. Bad doctrine leads to bad practice. Fanatical views of the imminence of Christ's second coming can lead to a host of errors, including failing to obey the injunctions of God in personal, family, and public life. We do not know the day when Christ will return, and we must live as faithful servants every day, ready to meet the Master. Whether or not you work for a paycheck, what "jobs" has the Lord assigned to you? Why is it important for the Lord's honor and your good that you work hard at them?

2. When professing Christians behave badly, it is sometimes our duty to withdraw ourselves from them (v. 6), to refuse to have fellowship with them (v. 14), and to give them a brotherly admonition (v. 15). Breaking fellowship with professing believers is a solemn act of the church and should not be done lightly or without the leadership of the church's elders. However, when done rightly, the Holy Spirit can use it to turn backsliding Christians back to Christ and to awaken hypocrites in the church to their need of salvation.